To My Child

_____

With love from

_____

_____

Date

A FAVORITE

PHOTO OF

YOU AND ME

"Yes, I have loved you with an everlasting love."

JEREMIAH 31:3

Father's Memories
TO HIS CHILD

Featuring the art of THOMAS KINKADE

Written by Tama Fortner

NELSON

www.tommynelson.com

A Division of Thomas Nelson, Inc.
www.ThomasNelson.com

Dear Friend in God's Light,

In my life, three roles have challenged me to delve deeply into my faith and discover the very best person that I can be: They are artist, husband, and father. As I think about the relationships I've developed with my wife and four daughters, and with the greater family I've come to know through my art, I understand that these aspects of my life are not really separate and distinct. They interrelate in many ways as I strive to "let my light shine" as God intends.

I have, for instance, shared my great passion—my art—with Nanette and the girls. From the time that Merritt, Chandler, Winsor, and little Everett first made their wide-eyed way into my studio, I've set up easels and canvases for them and allowed them to make very modest additions to some of my paintings. I've never pushed my art on them, but I'm proud to say that the older girls have picked up paints and brush and displayed some real talent. And, of course, I've dedicated canvases to Nanette and the girls, and my playful, half-hidden references to family members are well known to my collectors.

But it's also true that being a dedicated artist, loving husband, and supportive father call for different strengths and tolerances. Father has always been the role that has given me the greatest opportunity to stretch and grow in my faith. Probably that's because in my own childhood, my mom really raised the kids. She did a wonderful job, but I resolved long ago that in my family, Nanette and I would share the joys and challenges of parenting as a team. I have come to believe that a father is a vitally important part of a dynamic family.

I've been fortunate in having had mentors who stepped into my life at important times and became like surrogate fathers to me. First Charlie Bell—a sign painter, ship designer, and all around philosopher—then Professor Glen Wessels—one of the giants in the world of Twentieth-Century Art—offered me the gifts of their artistic knowledge and their wisdom about life, when I very much needed that kind of nurturing. Further, Mac DeWater, our country pastor, taught me the art of depending on God daily as well as the joy of a home filled with love and creativity. They may be part of the reason why to me sharing my art is such an important gift to my children.

The Kinkades live busy lives, but Nanette helps me guard our private space, which is so important to all of us. She lets me know when the world is intruding too much on the time I have to share with my daughters. She reminds me that spending time with the children never limits me; it completes me. Perhaps that's the greatest gift of fatherhood.

God's blessings to all,

A FATHER'S LOVE

My Dearest Child,

From the moment I first saw you, my life changed. I've marveled at the delights of toddlerhood and the scraped-knee adventures of later childhood—knowing, through it all, that I was watching the making of a great person, a person of whom I'm so very proud. There have been piggyback rides and games of catch, endless rounds of "But why, Daddy?"—and sometimes even flaring tempers—as you stretch your wings toward independence. But most of all, my heart has known more love than I ever knew was possible.

I thank my God upon every remembrance of you.

PHILIPPIANS 1:3

Through this journal, I hope to give you an understanding of the person I used to be as well as the person I have become. I have tried to record my hopes and my dreams, at this time in our lives, both for you and for myself. I want to share with you some of the secrets I have learned about life, faith, and fatherhood.

From our first moment together, I have thanked God for you. Know that He will always watch over you, even when I cannot. And also know that I—and God—will love you forever.

Always,

_____

MY BIRTH

When and where I was born

My parents named me

What was happening in the world when I was born

The leader of the country was

The World Series champion the year I was born

And the LORD God formed man of the dust of the ground,
and breathed into his nostrils the breath of life;
and man became a living being.

GENESIS 2:7

My earliest memories

ABOUT MY FATHER *(Your Grandfather)*

My father's full name

When and where he was born

My father grew up in

His best story about growing up

_____

My favorite game to play with my father

_____

I always think of my father whenever

_____

Have we not all one Father? Has not one God created us?

MALACHI 2:10

FROM MY FATHER

From my father, I learned

The most wonderful thing about my father

My father's occupation

He sometimes let me help

My father's greatest gift to me

The righteous man walks in his integrity;
His children are blessed after him.

PROVERBS 20:7

Because of my father, I now

My father taught me that God

ABOUT MY MOTHER *(Your Grandmother)*

My mother's full maiden name

When and where she was born

My mother grew up in

My mother's best story about growing up

A favorite memory of my mother

And Adam called his wife's name Eve, because
she was the mother of all living.

GENESIS 3:20

As a child, the thing I liked to do most with my mother

I always think of my mother whenever

FROM MY MOTHER

The greatest lesson I learned from my mother

My mother's occupation

My mother's greatest talent

She encouraged me to

My mother's greatest gift to me

My mother taught me that God

"Woman, behold your son!"

JOHN 19:26

MY BROTHERS AND SISTERS

My brothers and sisters

The things we did together

Our greatest adventure growing up

"And in you all the families of the earth shall be blessed."

GENESIS 12:3

I'll always remember

As a child, my favorite family tradition was

MY HOMETOWN

As a child, I lived in

Our street was

My favorite place in the neighborhood was

My favorite community event

Glorious things are spoken of you, O city of God!

PSALM 87:3

Games my friends and I played

Someone from my hometown whom I admire

MY CHILDHOOD HOME

When I was growing up, our home was

My favorite place in our home

When I wanted to be alone

My favorite hiding place

The best place to play

Home was a place where I could always

Unless the LORD builds the house,
They labor in vain who build it.

A TYPICAL DAY GROWING UP

Growing up, I usually spent my days

My chores included

On winter days, I would

On bright summer days, I liked to

Remember now your Creator in the days of your youth.

ECCLESIASTES 12:1

A typical day for my father

A typical day for my mother

LIFE BACK THEN

An ice-cream cone cost

My favorite ice-cream flavor

Our family car(s)

The clothes we wore

The most exciting invention of the time

Rejoice, O young man, in your youth.

ECCLESIASTES 11:9

Popular things to do

MY PETS

The first pet I ever owned

My favorite pet

Other family pets

The pet I always wanted

Then God saw everything that He had made,
and indeed it was very good.

My favorite book or movie about an animal

My best animal story

SPORTS

My favorite sport

The sport I like to watch

My greatest victory on the sports field

My most disappointing loss

Let us run with endurance the race that is set before us.

HEBREWS 12:1

My all-time favorite sports hero

The sport that I enjoy with you

SPIRITUAL BEGINNINGS

As a child, my image of God was

My favorite Bible story

My favorite person from the Bible

My favorite religious holiday

People who helped me learn about God

How my beliefs have changed since I was a child

The LORD is good to those who wait for Him,
To the soul who seeks Him.

LAMENTATIONS 3:25

My Favorite Scripture Verse As a Child

_____

_____

_____

_____

_____

_____

EARLY SCHOOL DAYS

The first school I attended

Other schools I attended

My favorite teacher during my early school years

My best subject(s)

A school experience I'll always remember

My best friend(s)

I wanted to grow up to be

Teach me, O LORD, the way of Your statutes,
And I shall keep it to the end.

PSALM 119:33

HIGH SCHOOL YEARS

The school(s) I attended

My favorite teacher(s)

My best subject(s)

My friends

Popular fads

*Oh, the depth of the riches both of
the wisdom and knowledge of God!*

ROMANS 11:33

The "in" place to hang out

My after-school activities

MUSIC

The musical instrument(s) I enjoyed most

As a young boy, I liked listening to

During my teenage years, I preferred

Now, I enjoy

For your mother and me, "our song"

He has put a new song in my mouth—
Praise to our God.

FIRST TIMES

The first time I rode my bike

The first time I drove a car

My first car

The first time I shaved

To everything there is a season,
A time for every purpose under heaven.

ECCLESIASTES 3:1

My first job

With my first paycheck, I

My first time to live away from home

FRIENDSHIP

God tells us that true friendship is

The friend that I've had the longest

A friend who feels like a brother

The friend I wish I hadn't lost touch with

The friend who makes me laugh the most

The greatest gift a friend has ever given me

You are one of my best friends because

"I have called you friends, for all things that I heard from
My Father I have made known to you."

JOHN 15:15

ROMANCE

My first crush

My first girlfriend

On my first real date, we went

My first kiss

My first broken heart

Behold, you are fair, my love!
SONG OF SOLOMON 4:1

The funniest thing that ever happened on a date

TRAVELS

The farthest I have ever been from home

The best vacation from my childhood

My favorite place to visit

The most exciting trip I ever took

I have always dreamed of going

The best vacation I've had with you

The place I would most like us to see together

"The LORD your God
is with you wherever you go."

JOSHUA 1:9

MY FAITH

For me, God has always

I have learned that faith

I sense the presence of God when

"You shall love the LORD your God with all your heart,
with all your soul, and with all your strength."

I hope I have taught you that God

Always remember

Someone who teaches me about God now

My Favorite Scripture Verse about God

_____

_____

_____

_____

_____

_____

INSIGHTS

My greatest strength

One thing I like to do

The thing I love most about life

I can't help but laugh when

I am always touched by

When I think about the future

For we walk by faith, not by sight.

2 CORINTHIANS 5:7

FALLING IN LOVE

My first impression of your mother

I fell in love with her because

The thing I love most about your mother

I proposed by

I am my beloved's.

SONG OF SOLOMON 7:10

Over the years, I have learned that true love

For your own marriage, I pray

OUR WEDDING DAY

The day, time, and place we were married

Your mother looked

What I wore

58

My best man and groomsmen

My most vivid memory of our wedding

For our honeymoon, we went to

Who can find a virtuous wife?
For her worth is far above rubies.
PROVERBS 31:10

NEWLYWEDS

Our first home

Our first real disagreement was over

One thing we still laugh about

The most difficult thing to adjust to

"I will never leave you nor forsake you."

HEBREWS 13:5

The best thing about being married

THEN CAME YOU

When I first learned you were coming into our lives

Your mother's reaction

My most memorable experience as your dad

Your name is special because

....

When I first saw you, I prayed

....

....

....

....

....

A PHOTO

OF YOU

Behold, children are a heritage from the LORD.

PSALM 127:3

THE JOYS OF FATHERHOOD

The thing I love most about being your father

The most surprising thing about being a father

I loved teaching you how to

I have no greater joy than to hear
that my children walk in truth.

3 JOHN 1:4

One of my favorite memories of you

When you become a parent, I hope that you will remember

WATCHING YOU GROW UP

As a child, you

As you grew older, you

I was so proud of you when

You tested your independence by

The hardest thing about watching you grow up

My prayer for you is

"Blessed are those who keep my ways."

PROVERBS 8:32

PLAY TIME

Always remember to take time to play because

_____

_____

_____

_____

_____

Our favorite game to play together

_____

_____

_____

_____

_____

The hobby I enjoy most

_____

_____

_____

_____

_____

_____

_____

The heavens declare the glory of God;
And the firmament shows His handiwork.

PSALM 19:1

I would like to teach you

I hope that you will teach me

I have always wanted us to

CELEBRATING CHRISTMAS

Our first Christmas with you

On Christmas morning, you

My favorite Christmas tradition for our family

I remember one year when

Every good gift and every perfect gift is from above,
and comes down from the Father of lights.

JAMES 1:17

Our most memorable Christmas experience

MY DREAMS FOR YOU

When you were younger, I dreamed of you becoming

Now, my greatest dream for you is

Dreams are important because

"With God all things are possible."

MATTHEW 19:26

One dream you have made come true

One of the things I admire about you is

MY PROMISES TO YOU

As your father, I promise

_____

_____

_____

_____

Although we disagree sometimes, I will always

_____

_____

_____

_____

I hope that together we will

_____

_____

_____

_____

Let us hold fast the confession of our hope without wavering,
for He who promised is faithful.

HEBREWS 10:23

Promises are important to keep because

You can always trust God to

My Favorite Promise from God

_____

_____

_____

_____

_____

_____

MY FAVORITE THINGS

My favorite time of day

My favorite season

My favorite book

My favorite movie

A memento from my boyhood

"Do not lay up for yourselves treasures on earth . . .
but lay up for yourselves treasures in heaven."

MATTHEW 6:19, 20

Something that I didn't like as a child, but is now a favorite

That which I cherish most in life

QUIET TIMES WITH GOD

Through prayer, I have found

For me, the best time of day to pray is

My favorite place to pray

Prayer is important to me because

I know that God hears my prayers because

My ever-present prayer for you is

"And you will seek Me and find Me,
when you search for Me with all your heart."

JEREMIAH 29:13

My Favorite Prayer

_____

_____

_____

_____

_____

_____

_____

Thomas
Kinkade

SOMEDAY... *When You Are a Parent*

Being a parent

_____

_____

_____

_____

When you have a child, be sure to

_____

_____

_____

_____

Always be ready to

_____

_____

_____

_____

Show your love by

_____

_____

_____

_____

Every day I will bless You,
And I will praise Your name forever and ever.

PSALM 145:2

Teach your child to

WINNING AT LIFE

I believe that God gave us life so that we could

_____

_____

_____

_____

_____

To be a success in life

_____

_____

_____

_____

I believe you are a success because

_____

_____

_____

_____

_____

Now may the God of hope
fill you with all joy and peace.

ROMANS 15:13

When life is hectic and hurried, remember

My best advice to you

GAINING WISDOM

When I was a young boy, I believed I would

As a teenager, I just knew

As a new father, I believed

Now, I know

In the future, I hope

Happy is the man who finds wisdom.

AS I GROW OLDER

The things that I once believed were important

With each passing year, I appreciate more

One thing I wish I had done differently growing up

One thing I wish I had done differently as an adult

"Give, and it will be given to you."

LUKE 6:38

When I was young, I worried that

But now I realize that

FAMILY TIES

You and I are most alike in that

We are most different in that

The person you remind me of most

Family is important because

With your own family, I hope you

"But as for me and my house, we will serve the LORD."

JOSHUA 24:15

Our Family Tree

Maternal Great-Grandmother
— *Dates of Birth (death)* —
Marriage
Maternal Great-Grandfather
— *Dates of Birth (death)* —

Paternal Great-Grandmother
— *Dates of Birth (death)* —
Marriage
Paternal Great-Grandfather
— *Dates of Birth (death)* —

Maternal Great-Grandmother
— *Dates of Birth (death)* —
Marriage
Maternal Great-Grandfather
— *Dates of Birth (death)* —

Paternal Great-Grandmother
— *Dates of Birth (death)* —
Marriage
Paternal Great-Grandfather
— *Dates of Birth (death)* —

Your Grandmother
— *Dates of Birth (death)* —
Your Grandfather
— *Dates of Birth (death)* —
Marriage

Your Grandmother
— *Dates of Birth (death)* —
Your Grandfather
— *Dates of Birth (death)* —
Marriage

Your Mother
— *Dates of Birth (death)* —
Your Father
— *Dates of Birth (death)* —
Marriage

You
— *Date of Birth* —

Your Sibling
— *Date of Birth* —

Your Sibling
— *Date of Birth* —

Your Sibling
— *Date of Birth* —

Your Sibling
— *Date of Birth* —

A Favorite Photo of Our Family

PLACE
PHOTO
HERE

*"I am the vine, you are the branches. He who
abides in Me, and I in him, bears much fruit;
for without Me you can do nothing."*

JOHN 15:5

INDEX OF PAINTINGS